Withdrawn

J 551.3

$12.99

Show me Book, Inc
Summer reading

June 2014

Withdrawn

EXPLORING THE SCIENCE OF NATURE

The Nature and Science of
MUD

Jane Burton and Kim Taylor

Gareth Stevens Publishing
MILWAUKEE

For a free color catalog describing Gareth Stevens Publishing's list of high-quality books and multimedia programs, call 1-800-542-2595 (USA) or 1-800-461-9120 (Canada). Gareth Stevens Publishing's Fax: (414) 225-0377. See our catalog, too, on the World Wide Web: http://gsinc.com

Library of Congress Cataloging-in-Publication Data

Burton, Jane.
The nature and science of mud / by Jane Burton and Kim Taylor.
p. cm. -- (Exploring the science of nature)
Includes index.
Summary: Explains what mud is, where it is found, what kinds of animals and plants live in it, and how it can be made into bricks or pottery.
ISBN 0-8368-1943-8 (lib. bdg.)
1. Sediments (Geology)--Juvenile literature. [1. Mud.]
I. Taylor, Kim. II. Title. III. Series: Burton, Jane.
QE471.2.B87 1997
551.3--dc21   97-8479

First published in North America in 1997 by
Gareth Stevens Publishing
1555 North RiverCenter Drive, Suite 201
Milwaukee, Wisconsin 53212 USA

Printed in the United States of America

1 2 3 4 5 6 7 8 9 01 00 99 98 97

Contents

Words that appear in the glossary are printed in **boldface** type the first time they occur in the text.

What Is Mud?

Mud forms when soil mixes with water. Soil is made of grains of sand and dust that have been worn away from rocks. Soil also contains pieces of dead plants and animals. This **organic** material, called **humus,** is what makes soil a rich food source for various plants and animals.

Soil also turns to mud when animals trample at the edge of a pool of rainwater. Sand grains, dust, and humus mix with the water. When the animals leave and the pool becomes still, the heavier sand grains sink to the bottom quickly. But the fine grains and humus may take several days to settle, and a layer of mud forms on top of the sand. The mud contains most of the humus that was in the soil, so it is rich in plant food. But the constant trampling keeps any plants from growing at the edge of the pool.

Below: Citrus swallowtail and migrant white butterflies sometimes gather in swarms on the mud at the edges of rain pools. The butterflies sip rich, liquid food from the mud.

Opposite: When large animals, such as these eland and impala, drink from a pool of water, they trample soil at the edge of the pool. This makes mud in which plants cannot grow.

Mud by the Sea

Top: Glasswort, or marsh samphire, grows where few other plants can — on estuary mud flats.

A fast-flowing river is often loaded with soil that rain has washed off the land. Farther down the river toward the sea, the river flows slower. The sand it carries sinks to the bottom. As a big river gets closer to the sea, all that is left of the soil it carried is a fine **silt**. The silt gradually sinks to the bottom at the river **estuary**, a place where the incoming tide stops the river flow twice each day. This gives the silt time to settle to the bottom. A thick layer of mud forms at the estuary, sometimes into vast **mud flats**.

Right: Mud flats provide food and a safe resting place for birds. These black-headed gulls cannot be preyed upon by a fox because the fox would sink into the mud.

Left: The thick black mud of an estuary provides rich food for plants and animals. Cord grass holds the mud together with its roots. Little plants called spire shells climb up the grass out of the mud.

Estuary mud is an especially rich food source because it contains the remains of many small creatures. The mud is also very **fertile**, making it good for growing plants. Special **marine** plants grow in it. Their roots hold the mud together so the particles cannot be washed away. In time, the mud will turn into land.

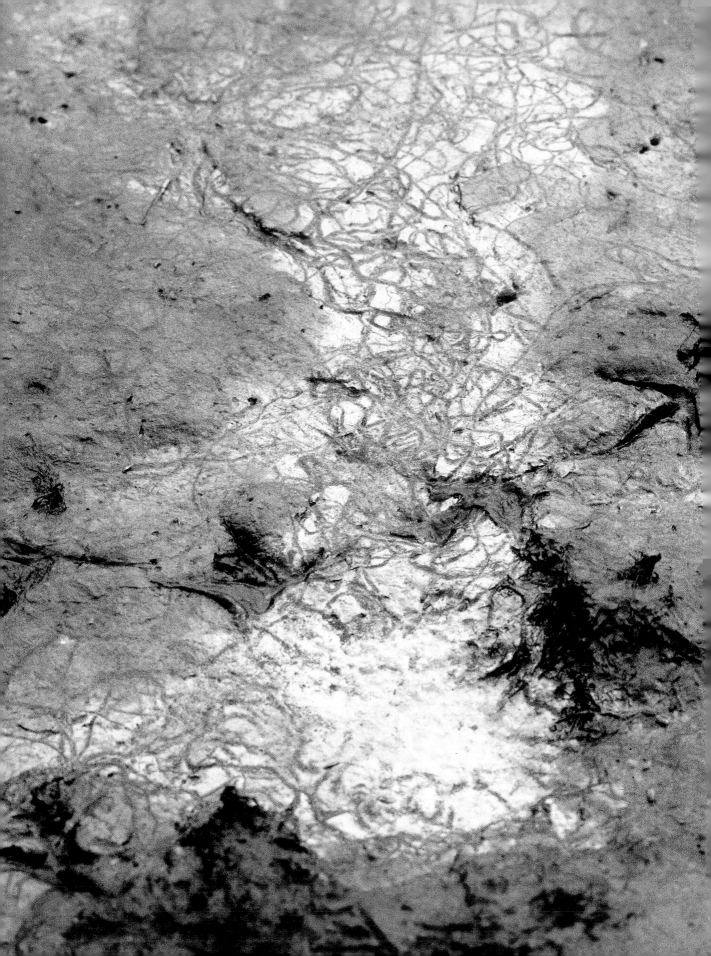

Smelly Mud

Mud is often black and smelly. It is black where there is no oxygen and the plant material in it has rotted. Only the very top of mud contains oxygen. This layer is called **aerobic** mud. Oxygen cannot reach the mud underneath this layer. The mud underneath is called **anaerobic** mud. Anaerobic mud produces smelly gases, including a gas commonly known as rotten egg gas. It also produces **methane**, sometimes called marsh gas. Natural gas that is piped into houses for heating and cooking is mostly methane. It probably formed in mud millions of years ago.

Only certain animals live in mud because there is so little oxygen in it. These animals have to come to the surface of the mud to breathe.

Top: A black, muddy **worm casting** from a lugworm.

Below: Midge larvae make their homes in mud. They are red because their blood contains **hemoglobin**, which is also found in human blood. Blood with hemoglobin is much better at absorbing oxygen than the clear blood of other insect larvae.

Opposite: This smelly mud was left when a pond dried out. A moorhen and various pond snails traveled across it and left their tracks. The shiny area where the snails crawled shows faint colors caused by **bacteria**. The bacteria in mud create the smelly gases. Bacteria can survive without oxygen.

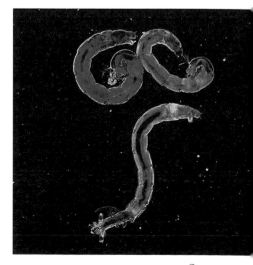

Mud-loving Trees

Top: A male fiddler crab scurries sideways.

Below: Mangrove trees have specialized roots that grow out from their trunks and then downward. These roots support the trees in the soft mud.

Soft, sticky mud seems an unlikely place for trees to grow — especially mud that is covered twice a day by seawater. But forests of small mangrove trees grow on tropical mud flats. Some mangroves grow even at the **low water mark**. Only the tops of the trees show when the tide is in.

Mangrove trees produce hundreds of **aerial roots** that grow 4-12 inches (10-30 centimeters) upward from beneath the mud. Aerial roots have many tiny **pores** on their surfaces through which the trees breathe. The pores are called **lenticels**. Mangroves need to breathe in this way because there is no oxygen deep in the mud.

Amazing tree-climbing fish called mudskippers live on the mud around mangrove trees. Some kinds of mudskippers grow more than 6 inches (15 cm) long. They hop over the mud after the tide has gone down. Mudskippers use their front fins like legs and climb up the aerial roots of the mangroves.

Above: Mudskippers climb out of the water onto mangrove roots and onto the mud. The fish at the top displays the fin on its back like a flag.

When the tide goes out beneath the mangroves, armies of fiddler crabs tiptoe out of their **burrows** in the mud. Each male has one large, brightly colored claw for signaling warnings and for fighting with other males. The other claw is much smaller and is used by the crab to put mud into its mouth. The mud contains many organic particles that are a good source of food. Female fiddlers do not have a big claw. Instead, they have two small claws that allow them to eat twice as fast as the males.

When crabs sense that the tide is coming in, they return to their burrows. Just before the water laps over them, each crab seals itself in its burrow by closing the entrance with a plug of mud. A pocket of air trapped inside the burrow keeps the crab alive until the tide goes out again.

Opposite: A muddy mangrove swamp is home to a large number of fiddler crabs. The crabs dig burrows among the roots of the mangroves. They come out to feed on the mud when the tide is out. The heron in the distance is probably looking for crabs to eat.

Below: The male fiddler crab uses its large claw to warn other males away from its burrow. If other males come too close, there may be a fight.

Below: The female fiddler crab has two small claws for scooping mud into its mouth.

13

Footprints and Beak Marks

Top: **Top:** Numerous shrimp can be found in estuaries.

The organic material in mud provides food for shrimp, worms, snails, and other animals that burrow in the mud. In turn, vast numbers of birds gather on mud flats to feast on these small animals. Ducks have beaks that are especially good for **dabbling** on the surface of wet mud to find the small creatures that live there.

Many kinds of birds known as **waders** also feed on mud flats. Waders range from tiny birds with short beaks that pick shrimp and snails off the surface to big birds with long beaks, straight

Shelducks swing their heads from side to side, leaving a regular pattern of beak marks on each side of their webbed footprints.

Small waders, such as dunlin, jab their beaks into the mud, leaving rows of little holes.

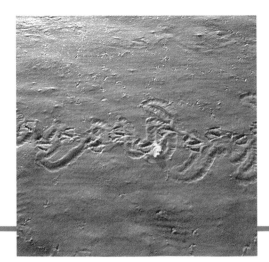

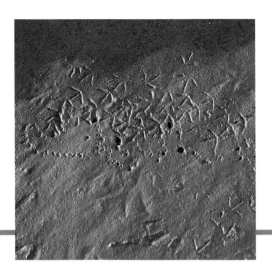

Left: Bar-tailed godwits are large waders with slightly upturned beaks. They wait at the water's edge until the tide goes out and then feed on the mud flats.

or curved, that **probe** deep for worms and shell-fish. Waders' beaks are so diverse in length that there is at least one type of wader that can reach food at every level of the mud.

Some birds that feed on mud flats leave a crisscross pattern of three-toed footprints. Round holes reveal where their beaks have probed the mud. Ducks leave webbed footprints and a regular pattern of beak marks where they have dabbled. Through careful study, it is possible to tell what kind of bird has left which tracks.

Minks leave well-spaced, five-toed footprints.

Dogs leave footprints with four toes spaced around a central pad.

15

Mud Nests

Mud is used by many different kinds of animals for making their nests or homes. When mud is wet, it can be molded into shapes. As it dries, it becomes hard and forms solid walls. These walls protect the nest or home. Bits of plant material mixed in makes the mud even stronger. Some animals mix in saliva, which makes the mud set extremely hard. Termite mounds (*right*) are made of mud mixed with termite saliva. When dry, some of these mounds are almost as hard as concrete. Chimpanzees eat bits of this termite mud as a medicine when they do not feel well.

Flamingos (*opposite*) make their nests from mud. They scoop mud with their beaks into tall mounds. In a hollow on the top of the mound, the female lays one egg. Both parents take turns sitting on the egg, keeping it warm until it hatches. The tall nests, which are located in shallow areas of lakes, keep the eggs and the sitting birds clean and dry. The thick, black, smelly, oozy mud all around the nests keeps the birds safe from enemies such as mongooses and jackals.

Left: Cliff swallow nests are made of blobs of mud stuck onto the roof of a cave or the under-side of a bridge. The swallows build a narrow tube at the nest entrance, just big enough for them to squeeze through.

Mud Baths

Top: As evidenced by their footprints, big and small cats lie in wait at water holes, knowing their prey will come there to drink.

Some animals in hot climates take baths in the mud. They do this because mud cools the skin. A layer of wet mud contains a large amount of water, and **evaporation** of this water cools the animals down. Just plain water would quickly dry, and the animals would soon be hot again.

When animals trample and wallow in pools of rainwater, they stir up the mud. Eventually, the mud settles to the bottom of the pool, forming a strong layer through which water cannot drain. This creates permanent water holes from which many animals drink.

Above: This African buffalo has been wallowing in red mud. Its horns and back are caked with it. While the mud is wet, the buffalo keeps cool. When the mud eventually dries into hard lumps and falls off, it may take with it some of the ticks that bother the buffalo.

Left: Warthogs live in family groups. They gather at pools of rain and roll in the mud until their bodies are completely covered.

19

Mud Cracks

Top: Over millions of years, mud can turn to stone.

When a lake or puddle dries up, it often leaves a layer of mud. As the mud dries, cracks appear in its surface. Sometimes the cracks divide the mud into squares — almost as if paving stones had been laid. Mud forms cracks because it **contracts** as it dries. As water at the surface evaporates, the particles of mud try to move closer together to fill space left by the water. This creates **tension** in every direction. But the more the mud dries out, the less it is able to stretch. And eventually, it breaks, forming cracks.

Right: Goats walked in this mud while it was soft. As the mud dried, the footprints were preserved and cracks formed. After the mud completely hardens, the goats' hooves will no longer sink in.

Dried mud makes different patterns depending on the type of mud. Here, a thin top layer of mud has cracked into small flakes, while the thick layer of mud underneath has formed large slabs.

The speed at which mud dries affects the pattern and size of cracks. The faster mud dries, the more it cracks and the smaller the cracks.

The first cracks to form in a drying **mud pan** are very long. The next cracks form roughly at **right angles** to the first. Once a crack appears, it continues to widen, so the first cracks are wider than the later cracks.

When mud dries out, the tiny animals living in it also dry out and die. But their eggs survive. They hatch when the soil becomes wet again.

Fossils in Mud

Opposite: A stone has been sliced in half and polished. **Embedded** in the stone is part of a bone from an extinct marine reptile called a plesiosaur. The pattern from the inside of the bone is visible. Below the bone is an ancient shell.

Imagine a big, muddy river flowing through a valley millions of years ago. It carries the body of a dinosaur that has died. The river flows into a lake, and the dinosaur sinks to the bottom of the lake. In the dark depths of the water, the body becomes a skeleton. In time, the skeleton is covered by layer after layer of mud. The huge weight of mud on top of the skeleton squashes it flat. The upper layers of mud press down on the lower layers so hard that all the water is squeezed out. Gradually, the mud turns to stone, and the dinosaur skeleton becomes a **fossil** embedded in the stone.

Many other types of ancient animals have fossilized in mud. But it is generally only the hard parts of these animals — their shells and skeletons — that remain. The soft parts of their bodies usually, but not always, rot away long before the rest of their bodies become fossils.

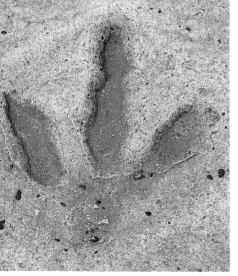

Left: The soft parts of animals usually do not become fossilized. But occasionally, footprints in mud, like this one from a dinosaur, turn to stone.

Mud is good for making fossils because it is soft and fits closely around a plant or animal. Because of mud, scientists are able to tell what animals that lived hundreds of millions of years ago were like. From fossil bones, scientists have been able to discover what the animals looked like. From fossil teeth, scientists can tell what the animals ate. From fossil footprints, they can tell how the animals moved. Even fossilized nests of eggs and babies have been found because they were buried in mud.

Below: Ammonites had coiled shells like those of snails. The shell on the right has been cut in half to show how it is divided into separate compartments. The animal lived in the large compartment at the end. There are no ammonites alive today.

Opposite: Soft mud from the bottom of ancient seas becomes a flaky rock called **shale**. Some shale contains thousands of fossil ammonites. The large ammonite pictured has been freshly exposed and gleams with **iridescent** colors. The colors will soon fade.

Glorious Mud

Top: A pumpkin plant grows in rich silt.

Opposite: Mud that is carried down rivers spreads over the land when the rivers overflow their banks. Mud is a natural fertilizer and makes the soil richer.

Mud flats are often thought of as wasteland. But mud flats are essential for the millions of tiny animals that live in them, for the birds that feed on them when the tide is out, and for the fish that feed on them when the tide is in.

Mud is also essential to some of the big animals — for cooling their skin and getting rid of ticks. Other animals eat mud as a medicine when they are ill.

Mud is important to people, too, because mud flats eventually become very fertile land. And mud carried by rivers fertilizes fields in many parts of the world.

Right: Hot water gushes out of the ground near volcanoes. This water will, at times, form pools of boiling hot mud that bubble and hiss.

Activities:

Playing with Mud

Mud or Clay?

Most kinds of soil are made of particles of different sizes of stones, pebbles, sand grains, and fine dust. Mud is different because all the particles in it are about the same size — very small. This makes mud smooth and creamy.

But there is another type of soil that feels like mud. Mud and clay are much the same. The only difference is that mud contains organic material, while clay contains only finely ground stone.

Baked Clay

Bricks are made of clay. Clay can be found under a few inches, or centimeters, of soil. It can also be found at the surface along streams where the topsoil has been worn away.

Collect a few lumps of this clay and keep it moist by wrapping it in plastic. Natural clay is often yellow or red in color because it contains iron.

Before using natural clay, it is a good idea to remove any stones and bits of plant roots that it may contain. Work the clay between your fingers to remove any of these items.

To make what is known as a thumb pot, form a ball of clay 1-1/2 to 2 inches (4 to 5 cm) across. With the ball resting on a flat surface (**A**), gently push your thumb down into the top of it (**B**). As your thumb goes down, rotate the ball slowly, all the time pinching the clay between your thumb and first finger to form the wall of the pot (**C**). If the clay starts to crack, use a little water to smooth it together. The end result is a small bowl, or thumb pot (**D**).

Leave your pot for several days to dry thoroughly (**E**). The clay will then be hard, but not waterproof. If you try filling the pot with water, it will just crumble into a heap of mud. To make clay waterproof, it has to be "fired," or heated. Heat produces chemical changes in clay that bind the particles together so that water cannot separate them.

People made this discovery many thousands of years ago when they put clay into a fire. Similar chemical changes take place when mud is heated by volcanic activity. The mud turns to hard stone.

Clay is fired in an oven called a pottery kiln. The clay has to be heated until it is red hot. When it has been fired and allowed to cool, the pot will be a different

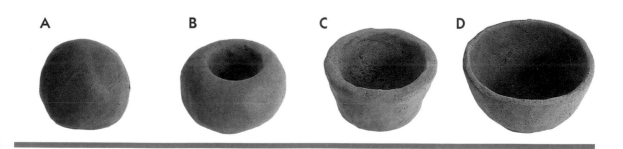

A   B   C   D

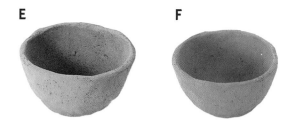

E   **F**

color than the original clay. Yellow clay turns to red pottery (**F**). Properly fired pottery is very hard and rings like a bell when tapped.

Warning: If you work with a kiln, have a knowledgeable adult help you every step of the way. Never put damp clay into a kiln or fire. Steam inside the clay may cause the clay to explode!

Track records

Moist mud or clay is fine grained and pliable. It is ideal for making impressions. When an animal walks across soft mud, it leaves perfect impressions of its feet, sometimes showing details of claws and even hair. But these footprints do not last long. Rain, wind, and sunlight soon smooth their edges, making the prints unclear.

To produce a permanent record of a footprint, make a plaster cast. You will need plaster of paris, water, a bowl or metal can to mix them in, paper clips, and strips of cardboard that are about 1 inch (3 cm) wide. An old spoon can be used to stir the plaster into the water.

The footprint that you plaster-cast should be freshly made and clear. (If you cannot find any tracks of wild animals, make a cast of a print that a cat or dog has made in the mud.) Surround the footprint with a ring of cardboard that is clipped together with paper clips. The cardboard will hold the plaster that you will pour over the print. Make the cardboard ring wide enough to leave about 1/2 inch (1 cm) of mud around the footprint. Push the ring a little way into the mud so that it stands securely. Pour enough water into the bowl to fill half the ring. (It will take a little practice to judge the right amount.) Gradually add plaster to the water, stirring all the time until the right consistency is reached. Then pour the plaster into the ring, and tap the cardboard very gently so that the plaster settles level.

Note: When mixing plaster of paris, always add the plaster to the water. Never try to stir water into dry plaster — it will start to set too quickly.

Plaster of paris takes five or ten minutes to set. After this time, remove the cast and wash it gently in water. When the cast is dry, write on the top in pencil where you made it and the date. Also write what kind of animal made the print. You can identify the animal by comparing the print with pictures in books about tracks of wild animals, or you could ask a knowledgeable person to help you.

Glossary

aerial root: a root that is located in the air rather than in the ground.

aerobic: containing oxygen.

ammonite: a type of sea creature with a coiled shell that was plentiful 100 million years ago.

anaerobic: having no oxygen.

bacteria: tiny, one-celled creatures that are found almost everywhere on Earth.

burrow: a hole dug in the ground by a small animal for its home.

contracts (v): gets smaller.

dabbling: the process by which a bird reaches into shallow water with its bill to obtain food.

embedded: surrounded closely by a supportive substance.

estuary: the point where a river widens and flows out into a large lake or the sea.

evaporation: the process by which water changes from a liquid into a vapor.

fertile: rich; a fertile or rich soil is good for growing plants.

fossil: the remaining traces of a plant or an animal that lived long ago.

hemoglobin: the red substance in blood that carries oxygen from the lungs to the rest of the body.

humus: dead plant material that is part of the soil.

iridescent: the rainbow colors produced when light strikes very thin layers of clear material.

larvae: the wingless, wormlike bodies of insects in their early stages of life.

lenticel: a tiny breathing hole in the surface of plant stems and roots.

low water mark: the lowest point to which the tide falls.

marine: relating to the sea.

methane: a gas made from hydrogen and carbon.

midge: a type of small, flying insect.

mud flat: a wide expanse of mud, particularly near the sea.

mud pan: an area of mud surrounded by land.

organic: originating from animals or plants.

pore: a tiny hole.

probe (v): to search an area with a pointed item, such as a beak or an instrument.

right angle: the 90-degree angle at the corner of a square or rectangle.

shale: the soft rock that is formed from layers of mud.

silt: fine particles suspended in or deposited from water.

tension: a pulling action.

wader: a type of bird that usually has long legs and a long beak. Waders often walk through shallow water to feed.

worm casting: the excrement of an earthworm.

Plants and Animals

The common names of plants and animals vary from language to language. But plants and animals also have scientific names, based on Greek or Latin words, that are the same the world over. Each plant and animal has two scientific names. The first name is called the genus. It starts with a capital letter. The second name is the species name. It starts with a small letter.

African buffalo (*Syncerus cafer*) — Africa 19

African elephant (*Loxodonta africana*) — Africa cover

American mink (*Mustela vison*) — North America, introduced elsewhere 15

ammonite (*Dactyliocerus commune*) — Jurassic clay, southern England 24-25

bar-tailed godwit (*Limosa lapponica*) — worldwide 15

Cape eland (*Taurotragus oryx*) — southern Africa 4-5

citrus swallowtail butterfly (*Papilio demodocus*) — Africa 5

cliff swallow (*Hirundo pyrrhonota*) — North America 17

domestic dog (*Canis familiaris*) — worldwide 15, 29

domestic goat (*Capra hircus*) — worldwide 20

dunlin (*Calidris alpina*) — worldwide 14

fiddler crab (*Uca annulipes*, male; *Uca dessumieri*, female) — North and South America, southeast Asia 10, 13

impala (*Aepyceros melampus*) — Africa 4-5

lesser flamingo (*Phoeniconaias minor*) — eastern Africa, India 16-17

lugworm (*Arenicola marina*) — eastern Atlantic coasts 9

midge (*Chironomus plumosus*) — Europe 9

moorhen (*Gallinula chloropus*) — Europe, southern North America 8-9

mudskipper (*Periopthalmus barbarus*) — Australia, Africa, India, South Pacific 11

pumpkin (*Cucurbita pepo*) — cultivated worldwide 26

red mangrove (*Rhizophora mangle*) — North and South America 10, 11, 12-13

shelduck (*Tadorna tadorna*) — Europe, Asia 14

warthog (*Phacochoerus aethiopicus*) — Africa 18-19

Books to Read

Amazing Dirt Book. Paulette Bourgeois (Addison-Wesley)
Animal Tracks. (Scholastic)
Beach Feet. Lynn Reiser (Greenwillow)
The Geography of the Earth. Susan Brooks (Oxford University Press)
1,000 Facts about the Earth. Moira Butterfield (Kingfisher)

Science Fun With Mud and Dirt. Rose Wyler (Messner)
Squishy, Misty, Damp & Muddy. Molly Cone (Sierra Club Books for Children)
Super Science Book of Rocks and Soil. Robert Snedden (Thomson Learning)
Wonderful Dirt! Peter Murray (Child's World)

Videos and Web Sites

Videos

Animal Tracks and Signs. (Encyclopædia
 Britannica Educational Corporation)
Estuary. (Bullfrog Films)
Marsh and Swamp. (Coronet)
Mud and Salt. (United Learning, Inc.)
Soil: An Introduction. (Phoenix/BFA)
Soil and Water: A Living World.
 (Barr Films)

Web Sites

www.earthsky.com/1996/es960207.html
ngp.ngpc.state.ne.us/wildlife/wrp3.html
members.aol.com/brandynjoe/fossils/
 index.htm
www.anglianet.co.uk/island/shotley/bird
 watch.html
www.discovery.com

Index